# *Our Parish*
# CHURCH

### Rev. JUDE WINKLER, OFM Conv.

**Imprimi Potest: Mark Curesky, OFM Conv.**, Minister Provincial of St. Anthony of Padua Province (USA)
**Nihil Obstat: James T. O'Connor, S.T.D.**, Censor Librorum
**Imprimatur:** ✠ **Patrick J. Sheridan, D.D.**, Vicar General, Archdiocese of New York

The Nihil Obstat and Imprimatur are official declarations that a book or pamphlet is free of doctrinal or moral error. No implication is contained therein that those who have granted the Nihil Obstat and Imprimatur agree with the contents, opinions or statements expressed.

D1636412

# GOD LOVES US

SIGNS of God's love for us are everywhere. When we walk outside on a beautiful spring day, we are led to think of God's love for us. We can also see God's love in our families, in the love of our parents, in our sisters and brothers.

A beautiful sign of God's love is our Church, God's family, the community of those who have answered God's call to follow Him. God called us to be a part of the Catholic Church because He loves us. Every time we gather together to celebrate the Sacraments, we are celebrating that love.

We also use the word "church" for the building in which the community meets, our *parish church*. Churches are filled with beautiful signs and symbols that help us to pray and to feel the presence of God. We are going to look at some of these to see why they are important for us.

One of the first things we see in our church is the *holy water font*. As people enter the church, they dip their fingers into water that has been blessed by a priest. They then make a Sign of the Cross with their fingers. This action reminds us of our Baptism when God cleansed us from our sins.

# THE CROSS

AS we look straight ahead, we see another powerful sign of our faith—a *Cross*. We begin all our prayers with a Sign of the Cross, such as the blessing we called upon ourselves when we blessed ourselves with holy water. The Cross reminds us that Jesus bought our freedom from sin through the Sacrifice of the Cross.

Churches usually have a large Cross hanging either over or behind the altar. These Crosses are so large that everyone in the Church can see them.

In Catholic Churches, there is always a statue of the body of Jesus hanging on our Cross. Some of these statues show Jesus Who has suffered and died, others show Jesus Who has risen from the dead. In either case, we cannot look at the Cross without thinking of God's love for us.

Very often, we see another Cross at the beginning of our Mass. As we sing our Entrance Hymn, there is a procession of the altar servers, the people who will read the first two readings, the deacon, and the priest. The server who leads that procession carries a Cross, again reminding us of the meaning of what we are doing, for the Mass is a celebration of Jesus' death on the Cross.

# THE TABERNACLE

A S we enter our church, we see a candle burning brightly as it stands next to a container called the *tabernacle*. The candle is a sign of respect. It pays honor to the presence of Jesus in the tabernacle. This candle is never put out as long as the Hosts that have been consecrated and have become the Body of Jesus are in the tabernacle.

This is the purpose of the tabernacle: it is the place where we keep the Hosts that are the Body of Jesus. From the earliest days of the Church, priests would consecrate extra Hosts during Mass. These were carried to those people who could not be present for the Mass because they were sick. There are also times when people can receive the Eucharist outside of Mass.

When we enter the church and reach the place where we will be sitting, we geneflect toward the tabernacle as a sign of reverence for the Body of Christ.

Some churches are built with the tabernacle in a small room on the side of the church. This room is dedicated to the presence of Jesus in the Eucharist, and people often stop in throughout the day to pray before the Blessed Sacrament.

# THE ALTAR

THERE is one thing that is the same in every Catholic church. In the front of the church, in a place where everyone can see what is going on, there is a large table that we call the *altar*.

This table reminds us that the first Mass took place at a meal on Holy Thursday. On that evening, Jesus gathered the disciples together to eat the Passover meal. During that meal, Jesus took the bread and said, "Take this, all of you, and eat it: this is My Body, which will be given up for you." He also took a cup of wine and said, "Take this, all of you, and drink it: this is the cup of My Blood, the Blood of the new and everlasting Covenant. It will be shed for you and for all so that sins may be forgiven. Do this in memory of Me."

Every time the priest repeats these words over our bread and wine at Mass, they become the Body and Blood of Jesus.

The altar also reminds us of the altar in the Temple upon which the priests of the Old Testament made sacrifices to God. This fact reminds us that our Mass is also the celebration of a sacrifice: the sacrifice of Jesus upon the Cross.

## CANDLES AND FLOWERS

N EAR the altar we place *candles and flowers* that remind us of the importance and the meaning of the Mass.

Most of us do not place flowers and candles on our tables at home for an everyday meal. They are used for special holidays, and they are a sign of how important and how good it is to be gathered together as a family. Meals are times when we not only eat but also share our love and concern for each other.

Our Mass, thus, is an important family meal. We are one family in Jesus, and during our Mass we eat our heavenly meal, the Bread from heaven: the Eucharist.

Flowers and candles are also used at another important time in our lives: when someone we love has died. Again, during the Mass we remember how Jesus died out of love for us.

The candle itself is another symbol of sacrifice. The candle sacrifices itself as it burns away in order to give light and heat to those around it—just as Jesus died to warm us with His love and to guide us with His light.

# THE SACRAMENTARY

AT Mass, the priest uses a book of prayers called the *Sacramentary*. This book is either held by one of the servers or placed on the altar.

Some of the prayers contained in the *Sacramentary* change from day to day. There are Entrance and Communion Antiphons, short verses from the Bible that the priest and people recite together. They are used when there are no songs at the beginning of Mass or at Communion time.

Other prayers are recited only by the priest. An Opening Prayer ends the Penitential Rite and introduces the Readings. A Prayer over the Gifts is used at the end of the Preparation of the Gifts. A closing prayer is used after Communion.

Some prayers in the *Sacramentary* are used every day and do not change. The *Sacramentary* contains all the words of the Mass with the exception of the Readings.

A central part of the *Sacramentary* contains the different Eucharistic Prayers that the priest recites. There are four prayers used during most Masses, as well as three others for children's Masses and another two for times of penance.

# THE LECTERN

THE first part of the Mass is called the Liturgy of the Word and takes place away from the altar. It begins with a Greeting and a Penitential Rite in which we ask God for forgiveness for our sins. We then have an Opening Prayer that speaks of the main theme of the Mass that day. After the Opening Prayer, we sit down and listen to the Readings.

These Readings are taken from both the Old Testament and the New Testament. They speak of how God has shown His love to His people throughout history.

After the Readings, the priest or the deacon preaches a Homily in which he shares his reflections on how God continues to love us and how we can love God and each other.

The community then prays together in the Prayer of the Faithful. We pray for the Church, for our government leaders, for the community, and for all of our other needs.

Most of the Liturgy of the Word takes place at the *lectern*. It is a large stand upon which the *Lectionary* is placed. It is as holy a place as the altar, for it is the place from which God's Word is proclaimed.

# THE LECTIONARY

THE *Lectionary* is a book of Readings for the Mass. Like the *Sacramentary*, it is treated as a sacred book for it contains the Word of God. Also, like the prayers in the *Sacramentary*, there are different Readings in the *Lectionary* for each day of the year.

There are Readings for the days of the week, Monday through Saturday. On these days, there is a First Reading taken from either the Old Testament or the New Testament; then a Responsorial Psalm; and then finally a Gospel.

The Readings are divided in a way so that they only repeat every other year. We call this a two-year cycle. Year one Readings are used when the number of the year is odd, while year two Readings are used when the number is even.

There are also Readings for Sundays and the great feast days of the year. On these days, there is a First Reading from the Old Testament, a Psalm, a Second Reading taken from the New Testament, and a Gospel.

Sundays have a different type of cycle for the Readings. It is a three-year cycle, with the years called year A, B, and C.

# THE PRESIDENTIAL CHAIR

IN addition to the altar and the lectern, there is one other place in the church where we turn our attention during the Mass. This is the *presidential chair.*

The priest who celebrates the Mass is often called the president of the Liturgy. He is chosen by God and consecrated by the Church in God's name through the Sacrament of Holy Orders. As the celebrant, he leads us in our prayers and helps us to apply the Word of God in our lives. He proclaims the words over the bread and wine that Jesus proclaimed at the Last Supper.

The celebrant leads the community in the same way that Jesus led His disciples: in service. He has the responsibility to do all those things that will help us pray better. In this, he helps to unite us as a family.

The presidential chair is not only the place where the celebrant sits. It is also where he begins the Mass with the Greeting and the Penitential Rite, and it is the place from which he proclaims the Opening Prayer and the Prayer after Communion.

# THE CHALICE AND PATEN

AT the Last Supper, Jesus used the cups and plates that everyone else used in those days. The cups were made from clay, and they looked a lot like our bowls today. The plates were even more unlike the plates we use today.

People used their fingers to take what they were eating. Also, they used the bread that was served to help them hold the food (bread in those days was flat and looked like pita bread).

Today, when we celebrate our Mass, we use a special set of dishes. The plate that holds the hosts that will become the Body of Christ is called the *paten*. The cup that holds the wine that will become the Blood of Christ is called the *chalice*. There is also a special cup that holds a large number of hosts. This cup is called the *ciborium*.

Because the paten and the chalice and the ciborium hold something so precious, the Body and Blood of Jesus, we do not use simple plates. Rather, we tend to use gold or silver for our celebrations, for these metals pay honor to the glory of God.

# GIFTS FOR GOD

AT the Preparation of the Gifts at Mass, two or three members of the community bring our *gifts* to the altar. There these gifts are lifted up to God, and we pray that God may send the Holy Spirit upon them so that they might become the Body and Blood of Jesus.

In the old days, people who went to Mass would bring all kinds of different gifts. These gifts were intended for the use of those in the community who were in need. They were also the support of those who were serving the community as priests and deacons.

Long ago, people did not use money as much as they do today. They would give their loaves of bread, their chickens, their bowls of beans, and whatever else they wanted to give to the Lord.

Because many of the gifts were a bit dirty, the priest would wash his hands after he had finished accepting the gifts. We still have the washing of hands, but now it is more to ask God to wash us free from our sins so that we can be worthy to offer the Sacrifice of the Mass.

Today, the gifts we bring to the Lord are our bread, wine, and the money that was collected from the community.

# THE MONSTRANCE AND THE THURIBLE

U SUALLY, when we want to pay respect to the Eucharist, we go to Mass. But once in a while we gather as a community to give honor to the Eucharist outside of Mass. We do this with our Eucharistic adoration.

During Eucharistic adoration, the celebrant places a large consecrated Host (which is the Body of Jesus) in a vessel called the *monstrance*. The Host is held in a small glass container so that everyone can see it clearly. The glass container itself is held up high on a metal platform (the metal is usually either silver or gold).

When we gather for Eucharistic adoration, we sing together, we read the Word of God, and we pray in silence for a while. Our Eucharistic adoration usually ends with a blessing of the community in which the monstrance is raised high in the form of the Sign of the Cross.

During Eucharistic adoration, we also pay respect to God by burning incense upon a glowing charcoal. The charcoal is held in a metal container called the *thurible* (or the censer). The incense that rises up to the heavens represents the prayers of the community rising up to God.

# THE BAPTISMAL FONT

M OST of the people who are baptized today are babies, but there are also older people who decide that they want to become Catholic. When babies are baptized, their parents answer all the questions for them, but when adults are baptized, they answer the questions for themselves.

Before someone is baptized, the person is asked to profess his or her faith. The community prays for that person, even asking the Saints to join us in our prayers. The person to be baptized is then anointed with a special oil to prepare him or her for the Sacrament.

The main moment of the Sacrament of Baptism takes place when the celebrant pours blessed water over the head of the person being baptized. He proclaims, "I baptize you in the name of the Father and of the Son and of the Holy Spirit. Amen."

This blessed water is stored in a *baptismal font*. It is a holy site, for it is the birthplace of the Children of God. After this, the celebrant once again anoints the person with blessed oil. Then he gives that person a piece of white clothing and a candle, symbols that the newly baptized person belongs to God.

# THE PASCHAL CANDLE

WE have another symbol of our rebirth in Christ. This is the *Paschal Candle*. On the evening of Holy Saturday, we bless a special candle that is the symbol of Christ's victory over death. This candle is used all throughout the Easter Season, as well as during the Sacrament of Baptism and during funerals.

The first symbol that we see upon the Paschal candle is the Sign of the Cross. The five points of the Cross are marked off with pieces of incense. These points, which remind us of the wounds of Christ and His terrible suffering, also remind us of the freedom from our sins that Christ bought with the price of His Blood.

Above and below the Cross are two Greek letters: the Alpha and the Omega. These letters are the first and the last letters of the Greek alphabet. Their meaning is that God created all things in the beginning and He is the God of all things until the very end of the world.

Finally, numbers of the year are written on the candle. This means that God is the Lord of all times. All of our history is filled with God's love, and every moment of our life should bring us closer to God.

30

# STATUES

ALL Catholic churches also contain statues of the Saints. Most churches have a statue of Mary, the Mother of Jesus. They also have a statue of the Saint for whom the church is named. There might also be statues of Saints who have a special connection with that community.

Saints are people who loved God and other human beings so much that even death could not conquer their love. They continue to love us from heaven, for they pray with and for us to God.

Our prayers are not addressed to the statues, but rather to the Saint whom each statue represents. The statue helps us to think of the Saint and to be assured that we are never alone, for the Saints are our friends.

At times there are candles before the statues of the Saints. The candles represent our prayers and our needs. We cannot stand before the statue all day long, but we can light a candle that represents us when we cannot be in the church. It is important to remember, though, that this is not magic. We are asking the Saints, our friends, for help, but we must also promise to become more like them—people who love God and each other.

## LET US GO TO CHURCH

ALL of this reminds us that our Churches are holy places. There we bring God the joys and the needs of our lives, and we receive the strength to go forward in God's love.

One of God's people in the Old Testament wrote of the joy that one feels when one goes to church. He wrote, "It is better to spend one day in Your courts, O Lord, than to spend a thousand elsewhere."